SPIRIT FLOOD

Jennifer A. Miskov, originally from California, moved to England in 2007 to follow one of her dreams of studying revivals. She wants to look at how to create a theology of living effectively through revivals so that years after these great moves of God come and go, people will still follow Jesus and live in true community. It was through her initial studies of revival that she came across Carrie Judd Montgomery and has thus decided to do her PhD exclusively on Carrie's life and theology.

Other Books by Jennifer A. Miskov

Silver to Gold: A Journey of Young Revolutionaries

SPIRIT FLOOD

Rebirth of Spirit Baptism for the 21st Century
In Light of the Azusa Street Revival and the Life of Carrie Judd Montgomery

Jennifer A. Miskov
With Bonnie Inkster and Rosie McNeil

Silver to Gold

Cover design by Affi Luc Agbodo.
Photograph of Carrie Judd Montgomery used
with permission by Flower Pentecostal Heritage Center,
photograph of Niagara Falls by Jennifer A. Miskov, and headshot by
Joanna Hield Photography. Photograph of Carrie F. Judd
inside of book is used with permission
by The Berry family.

Unless otherwise noted, Scripture verses are taken from
The Holy Bible: The New King James Version, (Nashville, TN: Broadman
and Holman Publishers), 1988.

Published by Silver to Gold
www.silvertogold.com

ISBN: 0-9842370-1-1
ISBN-13: 978-0-9842370-1-2

Printed in the United States of America and the United Kingdom

Table of Contents

Special Thanks

I am grateful to Allan Anderson for introducing me to Carrie Judd Montgomery for the first time and to Mark Cartledge for his graduate class on the theology of the Holy Spirit. Thanks also to the Foundation for Pentecostal Scholarship (www.tffps.org) for their support of my research project. I also want to thank Rosie and Bonnie for contributing to this work from their own experiences. Finally, special thanks to Affi Luc Agbodo for the cover design and for all his support in the Silver to Gold Project.

For Andrew

Thank you.
May God's recent word for your life come to pass in every way.
"For waters shall burst forth in the wilderness, and streams in the desert."
–Isaiah 35:6

"John indeed baptized with water, but you shall be baptized with the Holy Spirit."[1] -Jesus

PART I
Introductions

Seeds

Since being in England and studying revivals, the theme of Spirit baptism has emerged in my studies as I have looked at the work of the Holy Spirit in the early 1900's. This has led to my personal reflection on the subject. I was fascinated with this somewhat new theme for me which was central to the early global Pentecostal revivals of the 1900's. I had already had a deep experience in the Spirit over 15 years ago where I also spoke in tongues, but this whole language of being baptized and flooded in the Spirit was a new concept for me.

I became fascinated with Spirit baptism and how it played a crucial role in a great revival. I started pressing into finding out more about it through my academic studies and my devotional times. After attending a church service at a different church while here in England, in the midst of my hunger for more of the Spirit, the speaker talked about Spirit baptism. I was rocked by the Spirit that night and wanted more. I got home and was still on cloud nine after a sweet experience with the Spirit, when I looked at my phone before I went to bed. It was exactly 11:16pm. I thought it quite interesting that it was also November 16, 2007 which was displayed on my phone as 11/16. With the two 11:16's at the same time, I thought that maybe God wanted to show me something.

I decided to play a little game with God. I thought that I would turn to a book in the Bible and look up an 11:16 verse and maybe He would speak to me. I didn't want to have to look from book to book because then I thought I would be manipulating things. So I thought for a moment about which book to pick. Because I had been learning all about the Holy Spirit, I decided to look at Acts, which I was also going through at that time in my life. When I turned to Acts 11:16 in honor of 11:16pm on 11/16, I was in awe. I literally remember freaking out and saying "Shut up, God, no way, shut up!" which was my slang way of saying, "God, You're crazy, this is crazy!" In the midst of my journey to England where this newer theme of Spirit baptism was becoming a big part of my studies, where there was a growing hunger in my own heart for more of the Holy Spirit, and right after a talk about Spirit baptism, I read that night in Acts 11:16... "John indeed baptized with water, but you shall be baptized with the Holy Spirit."[2]

I absolutely love it when God is so incredibly real and present in our lives! Throughout the few years following that account, the theme of being flooded by the Spirit has continued to grip me. The upcoming essay is an adaptation of an academic paper I gave at the Society for Pentecostal Studies in March of 2010 in Minnesota. One of the main characters mentioned will be Carrie Judd Montgomery, whom I introduce first with a brief sketch so that you will have some context. Following the essay, I have asked a couple of present day women of God whom I know, the beautiful Bonnie Inkster and Rosie McNeil, to reflect and share their thoughts and personal stories with us. I pray that the enriching and Spirit-led responses they give will bless you indeed.

I honestly feel like I have just touched the tip of the iceberg in relation to the theme of Spirit baptism which I am still attempting to process myself. And while I admit that I am still wrestling with these things, at the same time and without a doubt I strongly feel there is something powerful when our heart's cry changes from "Lord, fill me" to "Lord, baptize me afresh with your Spirit." And this I pray, that the Spirit may do just that in our lives today.

Let me next introduce you to a friend whom I have never personally met, but whom I have grown to deeply value in my life. May her story enrich your life and increase your hunger for more of the Spirit.

Carrie F. Judd in Buffalo, New York in1866. Special thanks to The Berry family for their permission to use this photograph.

Carrie Judd Montgomery (1858-1946)

GROWING UP

During the same year and in the same state as the revival of 1857-1858, Carrie Frances Judd entered the world. Being the fourth of eight children, Carrie was born on April 8, 1858, and spent her early days in Buffalo, New York. During her childhood years, she had already faced the reality of both suffering and healing. She lost two of her sisters to severe illnesses and also saw her brother and father healed. Because of her own health, at fifteen years old, her brother invited her to live with him in another area of New York which had a better climate.

During her time there, she worked for an editor of a health magazine which would prove to foreshadow her later writing ministry. After a return home to help care for several sick in her family, she moved to another part of New York with the same brother. During her year's stay, she started a Sunday school with the neighborhood children. When she returned home, she was healthy enough to continue with her own schooling.

THE FALL

One cold winter day in 1876 as Carrie was walking to school, she slipped and fell hard on the icy ground. She continued to school that day but shortly after, her health began to rapidly deteriorate. Soon after the accident, on January 6, 1877, Carrie found out that she had spinal fever. What "seemed to be tuberculosis of the spine" developed into "tuberculosis of the blood" which forced Carrie to give up school and her aspirations of becoming a school teacher.

Being "prostrated with spinal complaint...the trouble extended to all the large joints. Her hips, knees, and ankles could not be touched, even by herself without great suffering." For over eleven months she could not sit up on her own. She could not even handle light or much time with people. She recalled that a small pillow under her head felt "like a block of stone." Her days in bed grew into months and then years. At a time when those around her were expecting her death at any moment and even her mother allowed friends into her room to say their last goodbyes, her father came across a unique article in the local newspaper.

The article told of the account of Mrs. Edward Mix, an African American woman from Connecticut, who was healed of tuberculosis through the prayers of Mr. Ethan Allan. Upon hearing this, Carrie asked her sister Eva to send Mrs. Mix a letter requesting healing prayer from her. To their surprise, the Judd family received a quick response from Mrs. Mix. The prayer found in James 5:15 was central to the letter as well as an encouragement to act in faith regardless of how she felt. Also mentioned in the letter was a specific time where both sides would pray simultaneously for Carrie's healing.

THE RISING
Even though no one showed up to Mrs. Mix's regular prayer meeting that day due to poor weather, she and her husband prayed for Carrie nonetheless. During their set apart time of prayer, on February 26,

1879, Carrie engaged in a spiritual battle. Finally, she felt it was time to act in faith and get up out of bed. She walked over to the nearby chair which she hadn't been able to do for some time before. Her skin color gradually changed from yellow back to pink and it was evident that her healing process was ignited from that day forward. By April of that same year, she was well enough to use the stairs and go outside to visit the neighbors. In the years that followed, she continued to correspond with Mrs. Mix. At one point Mrs. Mix even came to visit and they went out into the city to pray for healing of those who were sick.

HEALING HOMES

News of Carrie's healing spread and she soon became the talk of the town. People heard her story in newspapers and wrote letters to her asking if she was really healed. Many people came to her to hear her story and to receive prayer. Her compassion was stirred and in the summer of 1880 she opened up a room in her parents' home to receive such people. Soon after, she decided to open up a healing home in Buffalo, New York in April of 1882. This was one of the first healing homes in New York and was used as a model for many future healing homes in the country.

WRITER

Carrie was also a prolific writer. Based on the prayer found in James 5 and her own healing experience, she wrote *The Prayer of Faith* (1880) to encourage others to embrace and take hold of their healing. This book was significant because it was among some of the first prominent books written on the subject of divine healing in her time. In 1881, Carrie also initiated a magazine called *Triumphs of Faith,* which emphasized holiness and divine healing themes. She continued to write and edit this journal for over 60 years.

PREACHER

Carrie became an itinerant preacher and teacher and traveled nationally and even internationally throughout her life to share her story of healing and to encourage people in their faith. Her zeal to spread the somewhat unpopular message of divine healing at that time put her in the category of a radical evangelical. Through her close friendship with A.B. Simpson, she eventually became a part of the forming of the Christian and Missionary Alliance (CMA). Simpson continually encouraged and created space for her to step out and share her story.

Growing up in the Episcopalian church, Carrie transcended denominational barriers when she shared her story at Baptist, Presbyterian, Episcopalian, Salvation Army, Christian and Missionary Alliance, and other gatherings. She also organized Cazadero Camp meetings throughout the years which impacted many leaders from all different backgrounds.

Not too long after the Civil War and in a time before Martin Luther King Jr. came to the scene, she also preached to African Americans. In 1889, Carrie experienced some persecution and even some churches shutting their doors to her, first because she was a woman preacher and second because she spoke to African Americans. Regardless of these things, Carrie continued to share what God had done in her life to those who would listen.

WEDDING BELLS AND CALIFORNIA

In 1890, Carrie married a successful business man named George S. Montgomery who was previously healed of diabetes and afterward had "consecrated himself to the Lord's service." He brought her from Buffalo, New York to Oakland, California. With her husband's support, she opened up an orphanage and a training center in addition to her healing home.

The Montgomery's built the Home of Peace which is still there to this day. This was the first healing home on the West Coast even before John G. Lake's. Through Carrie's move to California, she was one of the early advocates of divine healing on the west side of the nation. In several histories of the Divine Healing Movement, Carrie is the only woman listed among the other key shapers in the movement: Charles Cullis, A.B. Simpson, A.J. Gordon, William E. Boardman, Andrew Murray, and other men. She and her husband also became honorary officers in the Salvation Army before the turn of the century.

THE PENTECOSTAL STAMP

When the birth of American Pentecostalism arose through the Azusa Street Revival in California in 1906, Carrie, although hesitant at first, eventually received her Spirit baptism experience (in 1908). Even at the age of 50 and having already been a successful minister, she was open to all that the Spirit had to offer. She claimed that this experience deepened her spirituality. As a result of this, the theme of Spirit baptism became integrated into her magazine and her teaching.

Because of her great reputation, she was used as a bridge between Evangelicals and Pentecostals. To the Evangelicals, she was a prominent voice to introduce Spirit baptism without all the fanaticism many times attached to it; and to the Pentecostals, she remained balanced in her views and didn't overemphasize the gift of tongues. While not cutting her ties with the other organizations she was a part of, by 1914, Carrie joined the newly forming Assemblies of God.

Throughout her life, Carrie was personal friends with Charles Cullis, A.B. Simpson, William Booth, Minnie Abrams, Pandita Ramabai, Elizabeth Baxter, Maria Woodworth-Etter, Alexander Boddy, William J. Seymour and was connected to Smith Wigglesworth, Aimee Semple McPherson, John G. Lake, and many other prominent Christian leaders in her time. She continued her ministry until her death on July 26, 1946 and was succeeded by her only child, Faith Berry.

INSPIRATION
Carrie continually gave away whatever she received from the Lord. After her own healing, she taught others about healing and prayed for them to be made well. She later lived through the Pentecostal revival of the early 1900's and was open to all that the Spirit wanted to do, while remaining balanced in the midst of some fanaticism. After her

Spirit baptism experience, she encouraged others towards the same fullness. Whenever she experienced something from God, she eagerly sought to help others receive the same. Regardless of already being successful in ministry, Carrie never wanted to miss all that the Spirit had for her. The way in which she approached revivals and newer moves of God with an open heart to receive all that God had for her, serves to encourage people today to do the same.

Carrie remained faithful to her husband and to the Lord all the days of her life. She lived a full life with total surrender to the Holy Spirit, unity in love, healing, fullness of the Spirit, and faith as prominent themes throughout. While Carrie made mistakes in her life like all people do, she serves as an inspiration, not only for young people and for women to step out in faith against all odds, but for all people to live lives fully surrendered to the Holy Spirit, to be unified in love above all controversies, and to freely give away what has been freely received.[3]

PART 2
Revival of a
Forgotten Hero

Rebirth of Spirit Baptism for the 21st Century

This essay will explore the significance of Spirit baptism as a cornerstone in early Pentecostal history and look at how its emphasis has since declined in Pentecostal and Charismatic circles. Based on Carrie Judd Montgomery's own Spirit baptism experience, I will present significant aspects or approaches to Spirit baptism that need to be recovered, the potential effects of that re-adjustment, and look at how Spirit baptism can be translated into the 21st century.

Rather than entering into theological debates surrounding subsequence, the gift of tongues as initial evidence, the purpose behind Spirit baptism, the different perspectives behind Luke, Paul, or John's interpretation of Spirit baptism, and other controversies, my methodological approach throughout this paper is purely historical. I am not attempting to look at theological themes surrounding Spirit baptism as much as I am mainly taking a snapshot of history and observing the effects and significance that this experience played and can play today.

Let me freely state that I grew up in the Vineyard Movement led by John Wimber (1934-1997) where he did share his thoughts on the baptism of the Holy Spirit from time to time. Because I may have been too young when he was leading the church, I have trouble remembering, outside of recordings and books, the degree to which he spoke on Spirit baptism. And while history[4] shows that Wimber did speak in relation to the subject, after his death and throughout my adult life, I don't recall hearing the phrase "Spirit baptism" much, if at all, from those who came after him. While I do remember there was plenty of prayer for being "filled" with the Holy Spirit and even specific and concentrated prayer for people to receive the gift of tongues, the terminology used at the Azusa Street Revival (1906) was somewhat absent from what I can remember from my own spiritual formation.

My admitted bias here is that I am seeking to see if there might be something from early Pentecostal experience that needs to be recovered and reintroduced, or reintegrated into more broad Pentecostal, Charismatic and Evangelical circles. Because Spirit baptism can be interpreted in many different ways, for the basis of this article, it will take on a similar definition to that which some early Pentecostal pioneers gave it of a distinct experience coming after conversion,[5] usually followed with the gift of tongues (although many early Pentecostals believed in initial evidence).[6]

1. Spirit Baptism: Once a Cornerstone

In 1906, G.A. Cook stated in an Azusa Street journal called *The Apostolic Faith,* that "To endeavor to help those who are sending in letters of inquiry to the Apostolic Faith office, asking how they may receive the Holy Ghost, the writer will state a little of his personal experience in obtaining this pearl of great price, the baptism with the Holy Ghost..."[7] In early American Pentecostalism, Spirit baptism was exactly that, the pearl of great price. A leading global Pentecostalism historian, Allan Anderson, recalls that in relation to Pentecostal fires spreading in the early 1900's, there was an emphasis of "mission flowing from the baptism in the Spirit."[8] The hype surrounding a deeper hunger for and a waiting for the baptism of the Holy Spirit played a significant role in global revivals. Most scholars would agree that Spirit baptism was a major thrust in mission in early Pentecostal history.

In reflecting on today's world, I wonder when the last time in a Pentecostal or Charismatic circle there has been a sermon about being baptized in the Holy Spirit or an altar call for that to happen.[9] When was the last time any of us attended a service and heard an altar call for those who wanted to receive their "personal Pentecost?" And regardless of my own stance in relation to the gift of tongues as initial evidence or not,[10] where are tongues today? They were everywhere at the Azusa Street Revival.[11]

A study done in 2006 which included 10 nations, shows that

49% of Pentecostals and 32% of Charismatics surveyed say they never speak in tongues.[12] For those Pentecostals who still stand strong in believing that tongues are the only sign of initial evidence for true Spirit Baptism,[13] does that mean for them that almost half of Pentecostals surveyed have yet to receive their Spirit baptism? And if baptism of the Holy Spirit was central to a worldwide revival,[14] why is that something that many American Pentecostal and Charismatic churches do not put as much emphasis on today? If many people believe that the Azusa Street Revival was a critical launching pad for the Pentecostal movement in America which is still affecting thousands even to this day, I find it interesting that many are failing to integrate it into their own practical theology.[15] I agree with theologian Frank Macchia when he says that he has "thus come to wonder if the relative neglect of the doctrine of Spirit baptism among Pentecostal theologians might not need to be reconsidered."[16]

It appears that what was once a significant part of a breakthrough generation has now faded in many Pentecostal and Charismatic churches.[17] Pentecostal theologian Stanley M. Horton notices that at Nyack college in New York, that after a revival broke out there in the early 1900's and people decided that tongues was not initial evidence, the people there stopped praying for the Baptism of the Spirit. He goes on to say that he hopes "that will not happen in America as a whole in the present century. If it does, missionaries from other parts of the world will be coming here to spread the truth and call for a new Pentecostal revival."[18] This is just one account where theological differences in relation to Spirit baptism may have caused decline in it being emphasized further. Additionally, in relation to the Azusa Street Revival, other possible reasons for decline may have been division from within,[19] a lack of love at times,[20] and disillusionment in relation to the gift of tongues.[21]

One must wonder what things in relation to Spirit baptism might be missing since its emphasis has been toned down. Yes, more training, equipping, and discipling is needed to channel these spontaneous moves of the Holy Spirit, but have Pentecostals and Charismatics, possibly because of overemphasis or past mistakes, lost their formative vision to seek Pentecost today? And if that is the case, what might they be missing out on? Or, does it look like something different now that we are in the 21st century?

Even Third Wavers and others influenced by the Pentecostal movement might do well to rethink the importance of Spirit Baptism to see if there are places today where it has been left out, to the detriment and less effectiveness of the churchgoer or the minister. It might be important to ask if being baptized in the Holy Spirit is a prerequisite for successful ministry and anointing, for cleansing and empowerment. Alternatively, if one is already successful in ministry, will this baptism add anything to them or their ministry or not? A look at the baptism of the Holy Spirit in the life of Carrie Judd Montgomery will be helpful in finding some possible answers.

2. Carrie Judd Montgomery's Spirit Baptism Experience as a Model

The most influential woman in the Divine Healing Movement in America, Carrie Judd Montgomery (1858-1946), had already experienced the Spirit in a profound way previous to her own Spirit baptism experience. As a young woman, she experienced a miraculous healing which empowered her for lifelong ministry. Before the heightened Holy Spirit stirrings in the early 1900's, she originally thought that her first healing experience with the Spirit on February 26, 1879 was her Spirit baptism. From that point on in her life, she had a very influential and forerunning healing ministry.

Carrie was in her late forties when the turn of the century came with the Azusa Street Revival in Los Angeles in all its glory, making headlines. Even though she struggled and walked cautiously towards the things that were happening at the beginnings of American Pentecostalism, she searched out this "Pentecostal baptism" for herself. Even with her profound ministry, she admitted that she "grew still more thirsty for the rivers of living water." She said that she knew she "had tiny streams, but not rivers."[22]

She proceeded to prayerfully seek God for the Spirit baptism experience that was popular at the turn of the century. She was also encouraged by her friend Lucy Simmons who had already experienced her own Spirit baptism. It was with that same friend, on Monday June 29th, 1908[23] that Carrie, at fifty years old, prayed for and received her "true" baptism of the Holy Spirit. Immediately following this overwhelming experience with the Spirit, Carrie spoke in tongues for nearly two hours.[24] Less than two months after the event, she recorded her account:

> For some time I have been thirsting for the fullness of the Holy Spirit's presence and power. At the time of my miraculous healing, when a young girl, I was first made conscious of the Holy Spirit's work in revealing Jesus in and to me. At this time a power to testify came into my soul, and the Word of God was wonderfully opened to me, so that He has greatly blessed my ministry in the Word since that time. This experience I have always referred to as the baptism of the Holy Ghost until a few months ago, when I began to watch what God was doing in pouring out His Pentecostal fullness upon some of His little ones. At first I was perplexed. I knew my experience, above referred to, was most real and lasting in its effects. How could I cast it away? Then I came to understand that I was not to depreciate His precious work in the past, but to follow on to receive the fullness of the same Spirit.[25]

Did Carrie get baptized twice in the Holy Spirit? Was her first healing experience just a "filling" of the Spirit? Was the second experience a deeper expression and maybe even a renewal of her first experience but with a different outcome? Even though she had already experienced the Holy Spirit's presence in her earlier healing encounter, she felt that there was still something more. Referring to the earlier quote, she experienced "tiny streams" but not yet "rivers." When some of her friends received their "Pentecost" experience and she noticed the transformations that took place in their lives, she began to hunger for something she never realized existed before.

Let's look at the mile run to get a better idea of her situation. Before 1954, nobody really thought that the mile run record could be broken in less than 4 minutes. No one even tried because that is where the bar had always been raised. It wasn't until Roger Bannister from England broke the record on May 16, 1954 that people began to realize that it was even possible. He ran the mile in 3 minutes and 59.4 seconds. Less than two months later, John Landy from Australia broke Banister's record for the mile run in 3 minutes and 57.9 seconds. Even today, sports experts regard Banister's achievement as one of the greatest athletic successes of all time. He broke a barrier that people didn't even think to break before. No one thought it was possible.[26]

It seems in the revivals of the early twentieth century, especially in the Azusa Street Revival, that the Holy Spirit broke down barriers, even racial ones, to bring in a new outpouring of the Spirit and presence of God that not many had been accustomed to before. While there were stories of Spirit Baptisms with speaking in tongues scattered throughout history, Carrie most likely did not come across anyone who had received the baptism of the Holy Spirit with the gift of tongues until the few years before her own Spirit baptism experience. When Carrie saw deeper expressions of the Holy Spirit for the first time, she was awakened in her spirit to hunger for something she never realized was possible before that time. Simmons was one of the first people whom Carrie observed first hand who broke the figurative "4 minute mile" record, or in reality, had her

Spirit baptism experience. Carrie admitted that she was at first somewhat skeptical of the "Pentecostal fullness," but after seeing the positive effects it had on her friend, Carrie was struck to the core; enough to embrace the experience for herself.[27]

If Carrie, who was already thriving in her ministry, previously believed that she had already been baptized in the Holy Spirit, one must wonder what greater affect her "second" baptism of the Holy Spirit with the gift of tongues following, had on her life and her ministry. After this "second" Spirit baptism, Carrie claimed to have experienced a greater increase of joy, love, power for service, "teachableness," love of the Word of God, and "fellowship in prayer and praise."[28] She described in a sermon a few years after, that her "fuller baptism" experience resulted in "freedom of the mind from all care," which she had previously yet to settle.[29] She also described her life following her Spirit baptism as one where she mounted up with wings and gained physical strength in her body.

Her baptism of the Holy Spirit also affected her ministry. Shortly after her experience, in her *Triumphs of Faith*, she became an advocate for Spirit baptism while continuing to maintain a balanced view that love was the best result of Spirit baptism.[30] Additionally, instead of just collecting money for foreign missions, she went on an international ministry trip. It was during the trip that she was first used as a bridge between Evangelicals and Pentecostals to introduce this new experience and bring some clarity and understanding to missionaries on the field. While it is highly probable that Carrie would still have been effective in ministry if she continued in her present state without her Spirit baptism, she claimed that the experience added new dimensions to her ministry.

If Carrie Judd Montgomery, an already successful and effective leader in the Divine Healing Movement and she being only one of many in a similar situation, saw significance in this experience, then what does that say for successful ministers who have hesitated to explore Spirit baptism? What about Christians who believe this Spirit baptism experience is not for them because it's too "Pentecostal"? Are they missing out on anything? Carrie would most likely say "yes" to that question. While from her example, Spirit baptism might not transform one's whole ministry, Carrie did claim that it enhanced her ministry in new ways and added a depth to her spirituality. It also empowered her for mission in a new way.

Whether it be Spirit baptism or a new move of God, Carrie's approach provides a great example for people from Charismatic, Pentecostal, Evangelical, and even other traditions to follow. She wanted to be open to all that the Spirit had to offer, even if it was not what she was used to. She believed that just because some people were fanatics in relation to this experience, this did not mean it was not from God or that it did not have value. She approached Spirit baptism with a cautious view making sure not to throw out the "baby" with the bathwater.

Present day Christians could follow her path to do the same thing today in regards to approaching new moves of the Spirit. The next time a strange phenomenon in relation to the work of the Spirit breaks out, hopefully people will be encouraged through Carrie's example not to miss out on all that the Spirit might have for them just because it comes in a "strange" looking package. Nestled in with all that dirty bathwater, there might just be a precious baby who is waiting to be seen. Regardless of how successful someone in ministry already is, by learning from some early Pentecostals, specifically Carrie Judd Montgomery, there's a flooding and overwhelming experience of the Holy Spirit available for all who want to take hold of it.

3. Spirit Baptisms into the 21st Century

We have briefly looked at the historical importance that Spirit baptism played in the Pentecostal revivals of the early 1900's, noticed how its emphasis declined through the years, and examined the significance of Carrie Judd Montgomery's Spirit baptism experience. It has been shown that Spirit baptism was a focus, a cornerstone, an experience at the heart of a worldwide revival. Now we will move on to discover the significance of the Pentecostal Spirit baptism for the 21st century and explore what it might look like when this theme is rediscovered inside, and even outside of Pentecostal circles today.[31]

Spirit baptism terminology in Pentecostal traditions is generally connected to one distinct experience.[32] I wonder what would happen if the metaphor and imagery linked to Spirit baptism was adapted to more than just that initial experience; if the motivation and the terminology surrounding the theme got applied after the initial experience as well. Once someone has received their distinct Pentecostal experience, it might be easy to settle, check that off the list, and then simply ask for more "fillings" of the Spirit after that.

I'm not saying that Spirit baptism experiences are invalid in any way. I am also not saying that we should seek multiple Spirit baptisms per se. But I am agreeing with T.L. Cross when he says that "If the Pentecostal reality is for everyone, then our terminology about what it is and how it is received must undergo theological reflection of a nature much more careful than in the past."[33] What if the Pentecostal Spirit baptism language was transformed and integrated into daily devotions? What if Pentecostals and others made "Lord, baptize me afresh in Your Spirit today" a *regular* prayer even after their initial experience? What if that longing found at the heart of Spirit baptism became a normal part of Pentecostal, Charismatic, and even Evangelical practice and language?

Looking at a pattern in history of God's work through the Pentecostal's Spirit baptism, specifically in Carrie's life, I notice that this theme could be explored more in churches that have hesitated in the past to receive this. Not to exclude those who haven't experienced this Pentecostal Spirit baptism and say that they are lesser but to create space to invite those who have yet to discover it to do so. There might just be even more that the Spirit wants to pour out in us if we just ask.

John Wimber echoed what was at the heart of Carrie's approach to Spirit baptism. In one of his talks when referring to Spirit baptism, he encouraged the people in his church to explore all the rooms in God's house. Metaphorically speaking he said that many Christians were "saved" in the bathroom and have spent their whole lives there without exploring the other rooms in God's house. Spirit baptism might simply be one room, salvation another, healing a different room and so on. He believed that there were many people, who because of ignorance and/or fear, did not realize all that was available to them in the house of God. He challenged them by saying, "Don't spend your whole life in the bathroom, enter into all that God has for you."[34]

Spirit baptism might just be one of the rooms in God's house that might need further exploration. The interesting thing is, many other traditions have at one time adopted this early Pentecostal theme and integrated it into their practices in years past, but have currently forgotten Spirit baptism today. There is a need to go back to one's roots and/or influences to find what was once precious and recover it. Broadly speaking for Evangelical Christians outside the Pentecostal tradition, rather than throwing Spirit baptism out or toning it down out of fear of overemphasizing one experience, what if in addition to the multiple "fillings"[35] of the Spirit that regularly get stressed, an honest look at the cornerstone of the Pentecostal revival was taken seriously once again? It is clear that there was something significant that took place in the early Pentecostal revivals in the 1900's that can be re-integrated into various other traditions today for possible similar effects.

Whether there is an agreed upon definition for Spirit baptism or not, whether it is accompanied always with the gift of tongues or not, at the heart of the early Pentecostal's Spirit baptism was a desire to be completely overwhelmed, submerged, flooded, baptized in the Spirit. Many people wanting that at the same time resulted in, or was the result of, the Spirit stirring up a revival. What if the whole theme and ethos behind Spirit baptism, that draw to be completely flooded in the Spirit, what if that imagery replaced or took a more central role in our hunger for the Spirit?

Regardless of whether we have already had an intense experience with the Holy Spirit or if we already speak in tongues, what if we prayed more regularly for God to "overflow" and "submerge" us; or even to "destroy" or "ruin" us in His Spirit?[36] Rather than desire to receive a "touch" of the Holy Spirit, or to be "filled" a little with the Spirit, why not pray to be overwhelmed, overshadowed as Mary was (Luke 1:35), flooded, baptized again and again in the Spirit so much that one is swimming in the Spirit? Why not move beyond asking for "tiny streams" and instead ask for "rivers of living water" to overwhelm us?

Spirit Flood

Lives that are continually submersed in the Spirit are empowered to face the challenges society throws and they can also liberate others through their overflow. How many times do we or people we know merely ask for drops in our buckets and receive only that, when if we were to hunger for rivers of living water, we would be flooded with the Spirit in that way? If I am to make any difference in this world, even after my initial Spirit baptism experience, I still need more than just a touch of the Spirit or continual fillings. I want my desire to be to swim in the rivers of living water, not just in one great experience, but on a regular basis. Think of what transformation might result when the desire found in early Pentecostal prayer circles, marked by an intense hunger to be overwhelmed, to be baptized in the Spirit, becomes a renewed prayer for Christians of different traditions today.

I close with the end of a talk that Carrie Judd Montgomery gave 100 years ago in relation to her healing and Spirit baptism experience entitled "Life on Wings: The Possibilities of Pentecost":

> Now, who is going to trust God for the winged life? You can crawl instead if you wish. God will even bless you if you crawl; He will do the best He can for you, but oh how much better to avail ourselves of our wonderful privileges in Christ and to "mount up with wings as eagles, run and not be weary, walk and not faint." O beloved friends, there is a life on wings. I feel the streams of His life fill me and permeate my mortal frame from my head to my feet, until no words are adequate to describe it. I can only make a few bungling attempts to tell you what it is like and ask the Lord to reveal to you the rest. May He reveal to you your inheritance in Christ Jesus so that you will press on and get all that He has for you.[37]

PART 3
Reflections

"More" by Rosie McNeil

How many times have you said to yourself "There must be more"? I had been a Christian and thought that thought for almost ten years before I began to encounter a type of Christian who had that "more"; more of something that I didn't understand and I couldn't put my finger on...more joy, more passion, more excitement, more intimacy with the Father, more life. I began to hunger for what I was seeing in the lives of these friends, which led me to a place of questing after God, seeking Him intently for all the fullness that He had to give me. I hungered to be in a place of hearing His voice, hour by hour and minute by minute, directing my days.

The discovery of the baptism of the Spirit really came for me during the Toronto Outpouring which happened in 1994. Shortly after our wedding, my husband Andrew and I travelled to Toronto to see what was happening there. I was initially apprehensive about what I saw. The weird and wonderful manifestations of the presence of the Spirit of God were unsettling and new to me. But in time, my hunger and curiosity got the better of me and I asked God to take away my fears and to meet me in a new way. He did this in a powerful, yet gentle way which left me changed and transformed, more in love with Jesus, more secure in the love of the Father, and not satisfied with anything less than a life where I could be truly intimate with Him.

Honestly, once we have encountered the Lord in this kind of way, we are truly ruined forever for anything less. All over the world in that season in the 1990's, the lives of believers were being radically transformed by a deep encounter with the Spirit of God. I learned not to look so much at what was happening to people on the outside, but to ask for the real stories of transformation on the inside, the healings, and the revelations of truth about who we are in Christ and the love of the Father.

And this is what Jen is talking about when she describes the baptism of the Spirit — it is a life-changing encounter with God, a saturating in His presence, a filling with Him that will utterly change the way we live our lives and the way that we see ourselves. It brings with it the "fullness of life" that we long for, the excitement of hearing the voice of God, and the boldness to follow through on what He says to us. Once we have tasted the presence of the Spirit of God touching us in this way, we are ruined for anything less. Nothing else will do.

Since that time, I have encountered the Spirit of God numerous times. Sometimes this happened gently, sometimes powerfully, and even sometimes violently, but always in a way that has led to more life and more knowledge of God, to more depth and more transformation. The Lord is always ready to answer our prayer for the "more" that He personifies.

What will it look like for you if you embrace God in this way? No-one can really say. But I can promise you that it will be good, that it will transform your relationship with the Lord and will change you more and more into the likeness of Jesus. We aspire to be like Jesus who was full of the Spirit and led by the Spirit (Luke 4:1). So go on...dare to ask the Father for the gift that He longs to give you and look to see what might happen.

And what if you have already received the baptism of the Spirit? Where do you go from there? Well, we need to stay in a place where we are more than just *open* to what the Lord wants to do, but where we are actively *hungry* for Him to move. For example, if I was to prepare a sumptuous feast for Andrew when he returned from work one evening and he said to me "Well, thank you darling, I'm *open* to eating that meal," that wouldn't communicate to me that he was particularly pleased or enthusiastic about what I was offering him. However, if he said "Oh darling, I'm so *hungry* to taste and experience all that you have prepared," that would be a different story and would speak of excitement and anticipation about what would be served!

Spirit Flood

There needs to be a constant cry in our hearts for more of the Spirit, a constant hungering in our spirits for more of Him, to experience all that He has to offer us. We need to cultivate in our lives a discipline of spending time in the presence of God, of soaking up life from Him and allowing Him to speak to our hearts and minister deeply to us. We need to practice and regularly use the gift of tongues so that our spirit can commune with and be refreshed by the Spirit of God. It's not always easy - so many distractions seem to present themselves when we are trying to carve out time in the presence of God. Have you ever sat down with your Bible to spend time praying, only to find your mind bombarded with tasks that need to be completed and a million other distractions? It happens to us all! And the answer is simply to write things down for attention later and resolutely press on into His presence.

I can guarantee that by cultivating a private life of intimacy with God in this way, we will find ourselves responsive to the Spirit of God when He moves; we will be able to speak and minister to others, ushering them into the presence of God too, in a way that is truly thrilling and fulfilling. And we will find ourselves really beginning to experience that abundant life that Jesus was speaking of when He said "I have come that they might have life and have it to the full" John 10:10 (NIV) or as it says in The Message "I came so that they can have real and eternal life, more and better life than they ever dreamed of." That's the kind of life that I want...don't you?

Fish Out of Water by Bonnie Inkster

So who wouldn't want a gift - especially a gift that is given from the Father? Jesus told His disciples to wait for the gift and that because of this gift they would have power to be witnesses, not just here but to the ends of the earth! So what was this gift and what kind of package would it come in? What was inside and when would it come?

The gift Jesus was talking about was to be delivered to them in a few days. The gift was the baptism of the Holy Spirit. Taken from *The New Strong's Concordance of the Bible* (1995), the word baptism here is *baptizo* in the Greek which means to overwhelm, to make fully wet, to cover wholly, to moisten or to stain. I love these definitions because for me each one states a truth. Take stains for example. When you stain something, you ruin it for anything else. The dye permeates the cloth and it will never be the same again. I know because I have never been the same again after I received this gift.

I grew up in the Catholic Church. I had a faith and I believed in God. I prayed and I knew that God could do the impossible - that which I could not. In 1976 at the age of 23, the Holy Spirit visited our family and "ruined," or baptized, us. My mother had gone to a mission and was directed by a friend to talk to a priest. He was wonderfully filled with the Spirit and my mother came home from that meeting baptized in the Holy Spirit. She then began to attend Charismatic meetings anywhere the Spirit was moving. My father went to one of these meetings where people there were also getting prayer for healing.

My father was like Cornelius in Acts. He was a God-fearing man but he also struggled to believe in what the Spirit was doing in those around him. At the end of this meeting they asked if anyone else would like prayer. He responded, "Well, if there is anything at all of this, I will get some prayer." So he sat down in the midst of this little meeting and people laid hands on him and prayed that he would be made whole. Absolutely nothing happened at that moment. Later on that night though, his ears started to drain and then four days later, even though he was 54 and being fitted for hearing aids, he could hear! And it didn't stop there, his back was healed, then his allergies, and then even his prostate was healed. He had experienced a Holy Spirit overhaul!

Well of course my parents shared this miracle with me. And a hunger, a desire, and a yearning for whatever they had received began to grow in me. I knew they had something more - something I didn't yet have. And the more I waited to receive it, the hungrier I got. I remember hearing my parents pray in tongues. I was fascinated by that and I so knew that I wanted what they had.

My husband Jim and I had gone away for a holiday and I woke up at about three in the morning to such a presence. I woke up Jim and told him that on our way home I wanted to check out all this Holy Spirit stuff. On our first encounter, we went to a meeting in a home and the Spirit was there in power. They asked if anyone wanted prayer and I jumped right in. The woman asked me what I wanted prayer for and I said, "Whatever they have!"

That very night I was baptized in the Spirit. I was overwhelmed, completely "wet," and totally "stained"! I fell to the floor and felt like I was surrounded by angels. I remember hearing a voice singing and then I realized that it was me; I was singing in the Spirit, in tongues! I was ruined for anything else in that moment. That power encounter with the Spirit of the living God changed the course of my life forever. Within a few months, my husband was saved and baptized in the Holy Spirit. In one year, 32 members of our families came to Christ and were Spirit baptized!

There have been other significant times and seasons in my life when the Holy Spirit has baptized me again with His presence, power, and passion. In the mid 1980's, we came in contact with John Wimber and the Vineyard Movement. At one point in my life around this time, I felt as though I was truly in a wilderness. My sister prayed for me and again the precious Holy Spirit overwhelmed me. I remember lying on the floor and hearing the phrase, "It will be like being born again, again." That week I found myself singing and rejoicing as the springs of living water gushed from within. I was fully "wet" with the Spirit!

Then again in 1994, the Toronto Blessing was thriving and the presence of God was thick. We were refreshed by the power of the Spirit. We continued to cry out to God saying, "God, we need more." The Spirit was tangible and sweet while at the same time powerfully dealt with the issues in people's lives while they were "under the Spirit."

Now I find myself calling out for the Spirit to come again and to baptize us afresh. Over the decades of my life, the one thing I know is that without the Spirit there is no life; but with the Spirit there is liberty, there is the kingdom of **God, His righteou**sness, power, and joy fully available to us. The baptism in the Spirit has caused a desire, created a hunger, and called forth expectation that only the Spirit can fill. Without the more of the Spirit in our midst we become dissatisfied and our affections turn to other things. We were created as spirit beings and we have a great need to be in the Spirit.

It is kind of like a fish being out of water. When a fish is fully submerged in the water, it moves freely and with ease, but outside of the water, it dies. Like that fish, we function best in the Spirit, fully "wet." The interesting thing is that we were not created for just life, but for life and that more abundantly. I don't want to be a fish contained in a gold fish bowl when I have the whole ocean to swim in. The Spirit is creating a hunger and thirst in our day for more. We want all that He has so let us begin to call out in one "accord" saying, "Come Holy Spirit - Baptize us afresh!" I wonder what that gift will look like when we choose to truly embrace it...

Closing Thoughts

Echoing the words of Carrie, Rosie, and Bonnie, I also pray that a hunger for more of the Spirit would increase inside of us, that our arms and hearts would be wide open to receive all that He has for us. May the Lord seal what has been highlighted to you through these words and may they inspire in you an increased and all-consuming hunger to be flooded by the Spirit again and again.

We don't want mere drops, Oh Lord, but send Your rain. Send Your floods of living water to drench us again we pray. Amen, and let it be so.

The Journey

Look out for more about Carrie Judd Montgomery coming very soon. To be notified of the release dates of these upcoming works in relation to her life, ministry, and writings, you can sign up to the mailing list on **www.silvertogold.com**. You can also access some of her original writings today at http://asleepinthedaylight.blogspot.com.

Additionally, to read a story that will help you overcome barriers that might be inhibiting you from receiving all that God has for you, check out the allegory entitled *Silver to Gold: A Journey of Young Revolutionaries* (available at www.silvertogold.com). The story is loosely based on Joshua and Caleb's journey; not of their escape out of the bondage of Egypt and into the wilderness of freedom, but from their freedom in the wilderness to moving into the Promised Land of abundance. This is a must read if you feel called to be a revolutionary for Jesus and you are truly ready to pursue that exceedingly abundant life (John 10:10/Ephesians 3:20) that He has already promised.

Silver to Gold
A Journey of Young Revolutionaries

Jennifer A. Miskov

About the Author

Jennifer A. Miskov is passionate about encouraging people to take hold of and pursue the abundant life Jesus promised. She has been involved in youth ministry and has discipled teens for over 15 years. In 2000, she lived with and served the poor in Mozambique and more recently she helped start Healing on the Streets for her church in the city center of Birmingham, UK.

Jen has preached internationally in Africa, Europe, South America, the UK, and the USA. She has also designed and implemented trainings, talks, and seminars on various topics such as discipleship, healing, living your dreams, team building, revival history, worshiping in spirit and truth, ministry, prayer, living a life of faith, and the Holy Spirit. Two of her life verses are John 10:10 and Ephesians 3:20 which come through in almost all of her messages and are major themes in her latest book *Silver to Gold*. She is passionate about inspiring people to move out of the comforts of an easy life and into the exciting and adventurous life of participating in the kingdom of God. She is available to speak or do workshops on any of the themes above. You can learn more about her and contact her through www.silvertogold.com.

About the Contributors

Rosie McNeil was brought up in the South of England and moved to Birmingham in 1989 to study for a degree in law at the University of Birmingham. In 1992 she met Andrew and they got married in 1994. Rosie practiced as a solicitor for several years before her two daughters Beth and Esther were born. Andrew and Rosie now lead Vineyard Network Church in Birmingham, UK and are the Vineyard Area Leaders for the Midlands. They are passionate about church planting, encouraging and developing new expressions of church, and training and developing leaders to use all the gifts and strengths that God has given them. Rosie particularly loves the ministry of the Holy Spirit and seeing people healed and equipped to face the challenges of life. Rosie can be reached through the church's website at www.vineyardnetworkchurch.com.

Bonnie Inkster is co-author with her husband Jim of *Tried, Tested, and True: 24 Secrets of Parenting* and they are both directors of Gateways Ministries International. Bonnie has a passion for the Holy Spirit and His prophetic expression. Prior to moving to the UK, Jim and Bonnie founded and pastored East Gate/Saanich Vineyard Christian Fellowship in Victoria, British Columbia. Since moving from Canada to the UK in 1999, they have started two leadership colleges. In 2003, Bonnie started a prayer ministry called Gateways Prayer Ministry to mobilize teams to pray in the nations of Europe. From

Spirit Flood

2003 to 2008, teams prayed in over 30 nations in Europe as well as Israel, Egypt and Jordan. In 2008, they moved to Birmingham, England where they are busy creating resources in the format of books and manuals to help people both in and outside of the church.

They have 4 fantastic children, 3 of whom are married to wonderful spouses, and 7 grandchildren. Bonnie and Jim are available for speaking engagements, seminars, and conferences. They are passionate about themes such as the Father heart of God, leadership, marriage, parenting, freedom, the presence of God, ministering with the Holy Spirit, the voice of God (prophetic), faith, prayer and intercession, maintaining spiritual vitality, and the kingdom of God. Bonnie can be reached at www.gatewaysministries.com. Additionally, Jim and Bonnie and Jen are willing to participate together in seminars and conferences.

Notes

[1] Unless otherwise noted, all Bible verses come from *The Holy Bible: The New King James Version*, (Nashville, TN: Broadman and Holman Publishers), 1988. Acts 11:16.

[2] Acts 11:16, *The Holy Bible: The New King James Version*, (Nashville, TN: Broadman and Holman Publishers), 1988.

[3] Most of this information for the biography has been found in the following: For accounts of Carrie's healing through her perspective, see Carrie F. Judd, *The Prayer of Faith* (Chicago: F.H. Revell, 1880; repr., New York and London: Garland Publishing, Inc, 1985), pps. 9-21, Carrie Judd Montgomery, *Under His Wings: The Story of My Life*, (Los Angeles: Stationers Corporation, 1936), pps.48-60, various articles in *Triumphs of Faith* and other journals, *TF* 27:2 (Feb 1907), "Songs of Deliverance," *TF* 16:3 (March 1896), *TF* 32:8 (Aug 1912), *TF* 35:2 (Feb 1915), *TF* 38:3 (March 1918), *TF* 39:2 (Feb 1919) and Carrie Judd Montgomery, "I am the Lord that Healeth Thee," *The Latter Rain Evangel* 2:4 (January 1910), 22. For public accounts of her story see, "The Efficiency of Prayer," *The Buffalo Courier*, November 15, 1881, "Disease Cured by Prayer," *The Sun* (New York), October 29, 1885, p.3. To see a reprint of the complete letter from Mrs. Mix to Carrie that was dated February 24, 1879, see Mrs. Edward Mix, *Faith Cures and Answers to Prayer* (Springfield: Press of Springfield Printing, 1882; repr., New York: Syracuse University Press, 2002), 38-39 (page references are to the reprint edition) and Carrie F. Judd, *The Prayer of Faith* (Chicago: F.H. Revell, 1880; repr., New York and London: Garland Publishing, Inc, 1985).

[4] These are from teachings on the Holy Spirit by John Wimber which were produced from the Anaheim Vineyard and captured on an undated c.d. My estimate it that they were recorded somewhere in the late 1980's, possibly early 1990's. It must also be noted that Wimber admitted that he changed his views in relation to Spirit baptism many times over the years.

[5] Frank D.Macchia, *Baptized in the Spirit*, (Grand Rapids, MI: Zondervan) 2006, p.78. Additionally, many believed Spirit baptism followed conversion and sanctification.

[6] Many early Pentecostals in America believed that the gift of tongues was the initial evidence, or proof that one had truly had their Spirit baptism experience. Many who grew in the Holiness or Divine Healing Movements later modified this stance to say that tongues was a sign but if someone didn't speak in tongues it didn't devalue or nullify their experience. When describing different people's views on speaking in tongues, Anderson says that "others like A.B. Simpson, Pandita Ramabai, Carrie Judd Montgomery, William H. Piper and some of the Holiness periodicals accepted that speaking tongues was one of the gifts the Spirit needed in the contemporary church, but that to insist on speaking in tongues as 'necessary evidence' of Spirit baptism was unscriptural." Allan Anderson, *Spreading Fires: The Missionary Nature of Early Pentecostalism* (London: SCM Press, 2007), p.53 and taken from *Live Coals* 5:6 (Feb. 13, 1907), p. 2.

[7] G.A. Cook, "Receiving the Holy Ghost," *The Apostolic Faith*, 1:3 (312 Azusa Street, Los Angeles: November, 1906), p.2.

[8] Allan Anderson, *Spreading Fires: The Missionary Nature of Early Pentecostalism* (London: SCM Press), 2007, p.14.

[9] There are plenty of churches that still speak along these lines and some that probably even overemphasize Spirit baptism to this day, but from the study that will be presented, there has been an overall decline.

[10] I Corinthians 13. Tongues as initial evidence that one has been baptized in the Holy Spirit is still a controversial issue in Pentecostalism to this day. Some who first believed in tongues as initial evidence changed their stance to believe that love was the true evidence. According to Robeck, Seymour believed in initial evidence of tongues only if it was accompanied with love in Robeck, Cecil M. Jr., *The Azusa Street Mission and Revival: The Birthplace of the Pentecostal Movement* (Nashville, TN: Thomas Nelson, Inc.), 2006, p.178.

[11] Jennifer A. Miskov, "Coloring Outside the Lines: Pentecostal Parallels with Expressionism. The Work of the Spirit in Place, Time, and Secular Society?", *Journal of Pentecostal Theology* 19 (2010), pps.93–116 to see a brief overview of some key characteristics of the Azusa Street Revival.

[12] Adelle M. Banks "Poll Says Many Pentecostals Don't Speak in Tongues" October 6, 2006, The Pew Forum on Religion and Public Life, based in Washington D.C., USA did a survey of the Pentecostal and Charismatic Movement in 10 nations. The survey Sample size: General public – 739; Pentecostals – 119; Charismatics – 421 http://pewforum.org/news/display.php?NewsID=11510 accessed December 16, 2009. It must also be noted that in certain environments, tongues is still prominent according to Donald E. Miller and Tetsunao Yamamori, *Global Pentecostalism: The New Face of Christian Social Engagement.* (Los Angeles: University of California Press, 2007). Their book demonstrates the flexibility of Pentecostalism to easily adapt to its surroundings while at the same time remaining true to its ethos and shows the other side of how in some environments the gift of tongues is still thriving.

[13] Many Pentecostals today do though, more than Charismatics, still hold on to tongues as initial evidence of the baptism of the Holy Spirit. Williams, J.R., "Baptism in the Holy Spirit," in Burgess, S., and Van Der Maas, E. (eds.), *The New International Dictionary of Pentecostal and Charismatic Movements; Revised and Expanded Version* (Grand Rapids, MI: Zondervan), 2002, p.358.

[14] Allan Anderson, *Spreading Fires: The Missionary Nature of Early Pentecostalism* (London: SCM Press, 2007), p.53. Anderson shows how at the Mutki mission in India and in many other places around the world, there were breakouts of Spirit baptism with people speaking in tongues and having similar manifestations, sometimes even before the happenings at Azusa Street. Though it is a very controversial issue to this day, for reference, I will be referring to the Azusa Street Revival as one of the main beginnings in *American* Pentecostalism, rather than Global Pentecostalism.

[15] Frank Bartleman, *Azusa Street: An Eyewitness Account* (Gainesville, Florida: Bridge Logos, 1980), a reprint of Bartleman's 1925 *How "Pentecost" Came to Los Angeles- As It Was in the Beginning*, demonstrates one person's perspective of some of the experiences that took place at Azusa Street.

[16] Frank D. Macchia, *Baptized in the Spirit*, (Grand Rapids, MI: Zondervan) 2006, p.26.
[17] "The Old-Time Pentecost," *The Apostolic Faith*, 1:1 (312 Azusa Street, Los Angeles: September, 1906), p.1. Spirit baptism with speaking in tongues has played a major part in the Azusa Street Revival even from the very beginning. See also Robert Mapes Anderson comments on this in his *Vision of the Disinherited: The Making of American Pentecostalism* (New York and Oxford: Oxford University Press, 1979), p.4.
[18] Stanley M. Horton, "Response by Stanley M. Horton" in *Perspectives on Spirit Baptism: Five Views*, Ed. Chad Owen Brand, (Nashville: Broadman and Holman Publishers), 2004, p.174.
[19] Charles F. Parham in 1906, Florence L. Crawford in 1908, then William H. Durham in 1911 tried to overpower William J. Seymour in different ways to take a bigger piece of the pie. Then Crawford stole the addresses to Seymour's *The Apostolic Faith* via Clara Lum and branched out on her own, and even later tried to steal the name of the mission. Then, even another white person, Durham, came to Seymour's church by his invitation, and while Seymour was gone, completely undermined him and tried to take over his church. So despite the opposition from outside of the Azusa Street mission, even from within, there was much conflict and heartache. Cecil M. Robeck, Jr., *The Azusa Street Mission and Revival: The Birthplace of the Pentecostal Movement* (Nashville, TN: Thomas Nelson, Inc.), 2006, p.318 and Allan Anderson, *An Introduction to Pentecostalism: Global Charismatic Christianity* (Cambridge: Cambridge University Press), 2004, p.35.
[20] Glenn A. Cook, a critic who turned in favor of Seymour said it well: "If God's people would only come together and forget about doctrines and leaders whose vision is blurred by building churches and collecting tithes, having only one objective, and that is to be filled with the fullness of God. Doctrines and teaching have their proper place in the gospel plan but that overpowering, drawing power of the love of God must come first, and our present lukewarm condition is caused by a lack of this love that 'nothing can offend," in Cecil M. Robeck Jr., *The Azusa Street Mission and Revival: The Birthplace of the Pentecostal Movement* (Nashville, TN: Thomas Nelson, Inc.), 2006, p.313.
[21] Even the gift of tongues when it came out as other distinct languages, proved disillusioning for many as they were sent out within days, even hours after their Spirit baptism only to discover that in the foreign land they could not communicate effectively. Allan Anderson, *Spreading Fires: The Missionary Nature of Early Pentecostalism* (London: SCM Press), 2007, p.27. Also, Walter J. Hollenweger, 'Rethinking Spirit Baptism: The Natural and the Supernatural' in A. Anderson and W. Hollenweger (eds.) *Pentecostals After a Century: Global Perspectives on a Movement in Transition* (Sheffield, England: Sheffield Academic Press, 1999) and also Walter J. Hollenweger's *Pentecostalism: Origins and Developments Worldwide* (Peabody, MA: Hendrickson Publishers, 1997).
[22] Carrie Judd Montgomery, "'The Promise of the Father.' A Personal Testimony," *TF* 28:7 (July 1908).
[23] Daniel E. Albrecht, "Carrie Judd Montgomery: Pioneering Contributor to Three Religious Movements," *Pneuma* 8:2 (Fall 1986), p.110.

[24] Carrie Judd Montgomery, "A Year with the Comforter," *TF* 29:7 (July 1909), pps.145-149. It must be noted that she received prayer for Spirit baptism about a week before this and she experienced an increase in God's presence but without the gift of tongues. She placed the date of her true Spirit baptism alongside the time she also spoke in tongues.

[25] Carrie Judd Montgomery, "Miraculously Healed by the Lord Thirty Years Ago,"10 and in *TF* 28:7 (July 1908), p.145.

[26] "Bannister's Four-Minute Mile Named Greatest Athletic Achievment" by David M. Ewalt with Lacey Rose in Forbes Magazine found at www.forbes.com/2005/11/18/-Banister-four-minute-mile_cx_de_lr_1118bannister.html in 2009.

[27] Carrie Judd Montgomery, "'The Promise of the Father.' A Personal Testimony," *TF* 28:7 (July 1908), p.146.

[28] Carrie Judd Montgomery, "A Year with the Comforter," *TF* 29:7 (July 1909), pps.145-149 and Carrie Judd Montgomery, *Under His Wings: The Story of My Life*, (Los Angeles: Stationers Corporation, 1936), p.170.

[29] Carrie Judd Montgomery, "The Life on Wings: The Possibilities of Pentecost," *The Latter Rain Evangel* 3:3 (December 1910), p.22 and also Carrie Judd Montgomery, "Life on Wings. The Possibilities of Pentecost," *TF* 32:8 (August 1912).

[30] Carrie Judd Montgomery, "Together in Love," *TF* 28:9 (Sept 1908), "'By this all Men Shall know'," *TF* 28:11 (Nov 1908).

[31] Robert Mapes Anderson, *Vision of the Disinherited: The Making of American Pentecostalism* (New York and Oxford: Oxford University Press, 1979), p.6, Frank Bartleman, *Azusa Street: An Eyewitness Account* (Gainesville, Florida: Bridge Logos,1980) which is a reprint of Bartleman's 1925 *How "Pentecost" Came to Los Angeles- As It Was in the Beginning*, Harvey Cox, *Fire from Heaven: The Rise of Pentecostal Spirituality and the Reshaping of Religion in the Twenty-first Century* (London: Cassell, 1996), Cecil M. Robeck, Jr., *The Azusa Street Mission and Revival: The Birthplace of the Pentecostal Movement* (Nashville, TN: Thomas Nelson, Inc.), 2006, and Allan Anderson, *An Introduction to Pentecostalism: Global Charismatic Christianity* (Cambridge: Cambridge University Press) all give insights to early American Pentecostalism.

[32] Stanley M. Horton, "Spirit Baptism: A Pentecostal Perspective" in *Perspectives on Spirit Baptism: Five Views*, Ed. Chad Owen Brand, (Nashville: Broadman and Holman Publishers), 2004, pg. 56.

[33] T.L. Cross, "A Critical Review of Clark Pinnock's Flame of Love," *Journal of Pentecostal Theology* 13 (1998), p.23 taken from Norbert Baumert "'Charism' and 'Spirit-Baptism': Presentation of an Analysis" in *Journal of Pentecostal Theology* 2004, pps.151-152 (147-179).

[34] This is from a teaching on the Holy Spirit by John Wimber which was produced from the Anaheim Vineyard and captured on an undated c.d. My estimate it that they were recorded somewhere in the late 1980's, possibly early 1990's.

[35] See Larry Hart, "Spirit Baptism: A Dimensional Charistmatic Perspective" in *Perspectives on Spirit Baptism: Five Views*, Ed. Chad Owen Brand, (Nashville: Broadman and Holman Publishers), 2004.

[36] Baumert states that "the noun 'Spirit-baptism' does not occur in Holy Scripture. The verb form of the phrase *baptizein (en) pneumati*, however, is a metaphor which is not to be understood in terms of 'to baptize', because the Greek verb has in itself different meanings (to submerge, moisten, make wet, shower, pour out on, wash, take a bath; to soak a piece of land, a cloth; to color, to glaze; to afflict, to destroy, to ruin)," in "Norbert Baumert "'Charism' and 'Spirit-Baptism': Presentation of an Analysis" in *Journal of Pentecostal Theology* 2004, pps.153-154.

[37] Carrie Judd Montgomery, "Life on Wings. The Possibilities of Pentecost," *Triumphs of Faith* 32:8 (August 1912), article was taken from an address she delivered at the Stone Church in Chicago in 1910 and revised by the author (CJM).

Why settle for silver when **you're meant for GOLD?**

www.silvertogold.com